I0133492

Poetry

for the

Soul

Uplifting Mind, Body and Spirit

Elois Fuller

PoetryandMusicfortheSoul.com

Copyright ©2015 Elois Fuller LLC
All rights reserved.

No part of this book may be reproduced by mechanical,
photographic, or electronic process, or in the form of recording, nor
may it be stored in a retrieval system, transmitted or otherwise be
copies for public use or private use – other than "fair use" as brief
quotations embodied in articles and reviews, without prior written
permission of the publisher and/or author.

This book is designed to provide information and inspiration to our
readers. It is sold with the understanding that the publisher and the
author are not engaged in the rendering of psychological, legal,
accounting or other professional advice. The content is the sole
expression and opinion of the author and not necessarily of the
publisher. No warranties or guaranties are expressed or implied by
the publisher's choice to include any of the content in this book.
Neither the publisher nor the author shall be liable for any physical,
psychological, emotional, financial, or commercial damages,
including but not limited to special, incidental, consequential or
other damages. Our views and rights are the same: You are
responsible for your own choices, actions and results.

This book is available at quantity discounts for bulk purchases and
for branding by businesses and organizations. For further
information or to learn more contact:
PoetryandMusicfortheSoul@gmail.com

Production: Parker House Publishing
www.ParkerHouseBooks.com

First printing December 2015

Printed in the United States of America

Acknowledgements

Special thanks to my husband, Jerry Fuller, for his love and patience throughout this process.

Thanks to Nancy Mathews of Women's Prosperity Network for helping inspire the writing of this book through her coaching from inception to completion.

A very special acknowledgment to my granddaughter, Valencia Gipson, who assisted preparing the material for print and is an awesome contributing writer to this book.

Thanks to my Apostles Ed Brinson and Yvette Brinson of Redeeming Word Christian Center International for equipping and enabling me to experience the true love of God through worship.

It would be robbery to neglect to mention my former Pastors, Willie and Grace Morman, of Fire Baptism and Truth church who was responsible for kick starting my spiritual walk of faith.

Thank you, All.

Foreword

Everyone has a message upon their heart to share, but few have the courage and commitment to share it with the world. You hold in your hands the messages and poetry from Elois Fuller. Beautiful and insightful words designed to inspire you, comfort you and engulf you in the grace and beauty of God's love.

Give yourself time to consume and appreciate each poem and you'll find deeper meaning and fulfillment with each verse.

Thank you, Elois, for listening to the still voice within and stepping out in faith and courage to share *Poetry for the Soul* with all of us.

~ Nancy Matthews
International Speaker,
Author & Global Leader
Founder, Women's Prosperity Network

Introduction

Though out life we all experience situations that affect us either positively or negatively. The poems in *Poetry for the Soul* were birthed out of the many obstacles I faced throughout my adulthood.

Being rooted in strong churches where faith and prayer is core, taught me to turn to the source of all help. Whenever I found myself down, confused or just needing a friend, God's word was always there consoling and assuring that his love never fails.

My prayer is that the readers of this book will find as I have consolation, uplifting and strength on a daily basis.

~ Elois Fuller

Table of Contents

I Am

I am the one who
Created the universe;
Formed man
From the dust of the earth.

I am the one who
Flung the stars in the sky.
I am the one
Who wipes the tear from your eye.

I am your bread when you're hungry,
I am your lover when you're feeling lonely,
I am God all by myself.
I am the one, there is no one else.

I am the one who supplies your needs,
Fights your battles,
Subdues your enemies;
Absolute Lord Adanijah.
Absolute faithful Jehovah.
I Am.

For You

We lift our voices to sing your praise
Like vapors they rise before your throne.
We sing out loud before the glory cloud
Showers of blessings all our own.

We come before you, Lord, with hands upraised.
In seeking your face we offer praise.
But in your presence we find so much more,
Salvation, healing and blessings galore.

And so we dare not be content
With merely singing your praise,
But with our hearts we offer up,
It's not just our hands we raise.

Love Flows Like a River

Its beauty is admired by passers who engage;
Its strength recognized and respected.
Even though it takes, it always repays;
Like a river's flow perfected.

It breaks down walls and barriers,
Opens wide like an estuary
To those seeking, it's a carrier
Providing sanctuary.

Love's constantly adapting and changing
As through life it flows.
At times it can be raging
If it's affection is opposed.

Love flows like a river,
Exuberating and fresh.
Happiness it will deliver
If you are found enmeshed.

Love

Love...
Makes me feel safe and at home.
That's where I know nothing but I don't care.
That's where the world's orbit no longer matters.
Time doesn't happen.
Nothing is in living color.
Nobody knows how to talk because love
Is no longer a word.

With love...
You can't miss the signs
Or it'll become invisible right before your eyes.
It'll be right there but then all of a sudden it
becomes so small that not even vision can reach it.

Love...
It's so fragile and delicate
With miscommunication
It could be misinterpreted or terminated.
Love is like a chameleon;
Once we think we've got it,
It reveals a new aspect of itself.

Love is...
More than just kind and genuine and patient.
It's a word that demands to be felt.

The Story of Love

Love never escapes reality or imagination.
When you love, you want nothing else but love.
When love comes you can't contain it
So it becomes contagious and uncontainable.
It's passed out, passed down, passed all around;
But love is just what it is,
Love.
It's a word if you let it be
But a duty if you let it do its job.
Love can flip you over, turn you upside down,
Inside out, confuse you,
Won't misuse you,
Cause you're a product of your imagination
So on the count of three go.

Who Am I?

Am I the God defined me or the me defined me?
But wait ...
Shouldn't they both be the same?

God's definition is perfection,
But I see me as imperfectly perfected
So is that the same?

We're all made in His image
Though I'm unique,
But we're all unique
So does that make us the same?

Or does the different aspects of Him
Imparted into us make our differences the same?

Then what does that make me?

I'm not a mere human being,
I'm made in His likeness
Representing the trinity.

So now that I've discovered me,
Who are you and what makes you unique?

Just As I Am

God made me just as I am.
I may not be
Who you think I should,
I may not walk
As you thought I would.
I may not speak
Words you desire to hear,
I may not shiver
When you thought I should fear.

But know for certain
Just as you see me,
Others see you
And thought you would be.

Though my walk is not perfect
Doesn't mean I'm not perfect
I'm perfectly beautiful because
God made me just as I am.

Purpose

What is your purpose,
Why are you here ?
Do you even care to know?
You awake each morning,
Continue on your day,
Sometimes high, sometimes low.

What if most every day could be
A day filled with highs
And the lows you seldom see?
Then find your purpose, it's not far away
Not hidden in a dark corner
Or on a distant bay.

It's calling out to you
But you will not heed.
Purpose is running after you
Trying to fulfill your need.
If you stop, listen and don't let life deceive,
Your God given purpose will be perceived.

Abundant Life Package

This package may not be gold
But riches and wealth will unfold.
You may not be considered royalty
But kings and queens is your ancestry.

This package is not an MD
But healings you will see;
The postman will not deliver,
It comes flowing like a river.

So don't be afraid to sign up,
Let it fill your cup,
Accept this package today;
Abundant life package is free, no need to pay.

Prayer is Who You Are

Prayer is who you are;
It's not what you do.
You say. I pray.
I ask who are you?

When you enter in the room
And the eyes gaze on You
They see who you are,
They don't see what you do.

You say, what I do is me.
I say, it's a product of you.
If you're a prayer it's who you are,
It's not what you do.

His Ears Are Always Open

His ears are always open
No matter where you are,
You may be high or low
You may be near or far.

No need to set up shop
In a foreign land
Nor think you can't be heard,
Because your prayer wasn't planned.

While in a business venture
Struggling to get ahead
Or nonchalantly going along
Without a thought of dread;

The very moment you stop and turn
Your heart to relay
The sincere thoughts within,
He will hear you as you pray.

His ears are always open
Never accusing or angry.
Remember, His pleasure is to answer,
Even your faintest plea.

Revelation

How do you know which way to go?
How can you tell when to turn?
How can you see beyond the door?
How can you, you're not learned.

How do you keep climbing
When others are falling down?
What's your secret, pray tell,
You're the talk of the town.

Some say this and some say that,
Some don't know what to say;
I can see you wear many hats
On any given day.

How do you know which way to go?
Please tell, I must receive,
Curiosity is aching me so
From my head down to my knees.

If you must know, I will reveal.
It's not my education.
To you that ask and all that will,
It's no secret, its revelation.

Sister

I know you've had ups and downs,
Who hasn't?
I know life's sometimes made you frown,
Who hasn't?
I know you've often wanted to give in,
Who hasn't?
But you are still here,
Strong, courageous and beautiful.

You've taken life's ups and downs,
You've smiled when you wanted to frown,
You never gave up nor caved in.
You are
Strong courageous and beautiful.
Now, walk in it!

Thoughts

Every thought is a creation
Waiting to be spoken.
Know your edge and begin to create.
Masked behind the ridiculous is often
The incredible,
Move out don't hesitate.

Your revelation
Becomes a blessing
For others when you release.
Great wealth has been transformed
From thoughts that do not cease.

So, from the moment you awake
'Til the time to lay down,
Don't cease to remember;
A single thought projected
Can release all bounds.

Christ the Rock

Lead me to the rock
That is higher than I
That I may bask in His presence,
That I may convert under his wings.
You are Lord, my God, my Rock.

Lead me to the Rock of Salvation,
The Rock of Refuge,
The Rock of Strength;
Upon this rock your word is established.
Christ is Lord, Christ is the Rock.

I will sing unto the Lord
A new song,
He is our rock, our refuge, our strength.
In His presence we find consolation.
Christ is the everlasting Rock.

You're Better Than That

Mere words cannot convey
The awesomeness you display.
Our minds cannot conceive
The vastness of your glory.

We lift our hands in praise,
Open our mouths to say
How much we love you,
How much we adore you.

We say you're awesome
But you're better than that.
We say you're mighty
But you're better than that.

We call you holy
But you're more than that.
We say you're faithful
But you're more than that.

You are, yes you are
Better than that.

Precious Lamb of God

Holy one of Israel, precious Lamb of God,
Draw me closer to your grace;
Cause my heart to receive your word,
Holy one of Israel, precious Lamb of God.

Make our hearts at one with you,
Create our spirits anew.
Let your light shine through,
Precious Lamb of God

Lead me to your throne on high,
Let your love perfect my life,
Holy one of Israel, precious Lamb of God.

You are the majestic one,
God's only begotten son;
Humbled, exalted one,
Precious Lamb of God,
The many breasted one,
Holy, redemptive one,
Merciful and mighty one,
Precious Lamb of God

Holy one of Israel, precious Lamb of God.

Bearing Everything I Need

You are my warmth on a cold, cold night.
You are my healer when I'm not feeling right.
Life's not worth living if I didn't have you,
You're bearing everything I need.

I would have nothing if I didn't have you,
Life would be hopeless without a clue.
There is no reason to go on without you,
You're bearing everything I need.

When I need love you are there.
When I need a friend, you let me know you care.
When I'm hurting you are there,
You're bearing everything I need.

Let Your Glory Rest Upon Me

Let your glory rest upon my glory,
Let your glory overshadow my will,
Let your glory saturate every part of me,
Let your glory rest upon me.

I will seek you with all my heart,
Let your favor go before me,
Forever Lord, I will follow after thee.
Let your glory rest upon me.

With a heart that's open to hear your every call
I will hearken unto you,
I will forsake all.
Let your Glory rest upon me.

Stand

You can run through a troop,
You can leap over a wall.
He'll raise you above your enemies;
The Lord will never let you fall.

Stand on his promises,
Stand in his love,
Stand in his faith,
Stand strong in God above.

Stand.

Rejoice

What do you do when trouble's pressing you?
Rejoice!
Rejoice in all your trials,
Rejoice through all your pain.
Lift your hands and praise him,
Shout hallelujah to the King of Kings!

What do you do when trouble's pressing you?
Rejoice!
Rejoice in all your labors,
Rejoice through all your tests,
Cry out to the Lord.
God is faithful to do the rest
So you can Rejoice!

Let Your Light Shine

You are the light of the world
And a light is not hidden
But it shines for the world to see.
Let your light shine
Bright for the world to see me in you.
Let your light shine bright for the world to see.

The world is groping around in darkness
Searching for the light.
Where is the light?
Light of the world
Let your light shine.

That's My Harvest

Hey! That's my harvest!
And I'm taking it back!

I'm giving you notice as a child of the King,
This is my now season and I'm preparing to reign.
Hey! That's my harvest,
It belongs to me;
Prepare to surrender,
To my voice give heed.

I'm taking it back!

Everything you've stolen,
It belongs to me.
I'm coming forth claiming victory.
Riches and treasures, family too,
You've had them long enough, Satan,
It's time for your due.

I've sowed for this harvest,
Now it's time to reap.
It's my now season
And I'm playing for keeps!

Hey! That's my harvest!

Overflow

Awake O' north wind
Come thou south,
Blow upon our garden
That the spices may flow out.

Overflowing,
Destroying every yoke
With the sweet smelling
Savior of our Lord.

The mountains bow down in your presence,
The birds a melody sing.
Calm our raging waters
As we welcome in the King.

Overflow with your anointing,
Overflow with your love,
Overflow with your goodness,
Overflow from above.
Overflow.

Only You

Only you can change the heart of man,
Only you can make him whole again.
Only you can make the crooked paths straight,
Only you could redeem the human race.

So we worship and give your name the praise,
We adore you O 'Ancient of Days,
Only you.

Only you can turn the dark to light,
Only you can change the wrong to right,
Only you can set the captives free,
Only you could deliver a wretch like me,
Only you.

He Love Us So

For a world lost in sin and shame,
He came down.
For a world clothed in unrighteousness,
He came down.
For a world scared in hopelessness,
Naked and bare, filled with despair;
For a world needing deliverance,
He came down.

And with a heart of love and compassion
Through forty-two generations,
He endured pain and suffering.
For a world that was lost
He hung on the cross.
He bore the thorny crown,
He could have come down.

But because he love us so he hung on the cross.

I was once a prisoner shackled to sin,
Clothed in unrighteousness, stained deep within.
He took away my filthy garments,
Washed me in his blood,
Clothed me in his righteousness,
Drew me with the spirit of love.
Because he love us so, he came down.

Soldiers in God's Army

We are solders in God's army,
Warriors of the King.
We're determined to make heaven our goal;
We will not falter against the enemy,
We are fighting a battle for our souls.

Now the battle is in array,
The enemy's taken his stand;
But as children of the King,
We have the upper hand.

Every stone that is thrown will crumble like sand
'Cause we're covered with the blood of the Lamb.

King of Kings

I will sing unto the Lord a new song
And his mighty works always proclaim.
I will shout it out upon the mountain,
Let the world know my savior reigns.

Yes, he is King of Kings
And Lord of Lords.
Of his mighty Kingdom there is no end.
He is Jehovah, God forever
Shall be, is now and always has been.

I will sing unto the Lord a new song,
I will tell of his mercy and his grace,
I will sing of his love and kindness,
Tell about the strength he gives
To run this race.

Yes, he is King of Kings
And Lord of Lords.
Of his mighty Kingdom there is no end.
He is Jehovah, God forever
Shall be, is now and always has been.

We're Grateful

We're grateful for your son
Dying on the cross,
Grateful for your angels
Keeping watch,
Grateful for your love
Eternal and true,
Lord, we're grateful to you.

Grateful for blessings
Flowing abundantly,
Grateful for unsurpassed peace,
Grateful for your faithfulness
Tried and true,
Lord, we're grateful to you.

Grateful for new mercies
Given each day,
Grateful for a heart to receive,
Grateful for cleansing us through and through,
Lord, we're so grateful to you.

Come Unto Me

Anytime I need an answer,
Anytime I'm feeling down,
You are there awaiting
With your arms open wide,

Beckoning.

Come unto me, I am the answer.
Come unto me, I will give you peace.
Come unto me, I am the only one
That can set you free.

When the weight of the world's on your shoulders
And all hope seems gone,
I have a faithful friend

And he's calling you to

Come unto me, for I am the answer.
Come unto me, I will give you peace.
Come unto me, I am the only one
That can set you free.

God Desires Praise

Everybody stop and listen
To what my God is saying.
He is searching for a people
That truly desires to praise Him.

He's looking for the pure in heart,
The soul that truly desires to praise God,
Not worrying about what the people say,
Not giving lip service as a kind of praise.

Not a mind that wonders in every way,
But a heart that's filled with genuine praise,
Be assured God's word is true.
Yes, he desires to bless you.

Don't just stand there making noise,
But with a true heart of worship
Lift up your voice.

He's searching for a people
That truly desires to praise him.

Jehovah Is the God I Serve

If you wanna know the God I serve
Just listen up, here's the word.
Don't need Mohammad,
Don't need Buddha,
The God I serve
He's more than enough.

He's Jehovah.
Jehovah is the God I serve.
The God I serve is an awesome God.
In times of need he's Jehovah,
Jehovah Jirah, that's his name.
The God I serve, he will never change.

The God I serve is a compensator
If you've suffered loss. He's Jehovah,
Jehovah Gmolah, that's his name.
The God I serve he will forever reign,
He's Jehovah,
Jehovah is the God I serve.

An Awesome God

When I think of how you brought me out
My soul wants to jump and shout.
When I think of what you've done for me,
How you've set my soul free,

I cry Glory! What an awesome God!

When I think of your mercy and grace
It gives me strength to run this race.
When I think of your power and might
And how your angels protect me
Both day and night,

I cry Glory! What an awesome God!

For Such a Time as This

We've been called into the kingdom
For such a time as this.

Called out of darkness
Into his marvelous light,
Called into righteousness,
Into the newness of life.
Sanctified vessels walking upright,
We've been called into the kingdom
For such a time as this.

All of creation has been anxiously waiting,
Anticipating our awakening.
As vessels of honor, we rise to the call.
With sword in hand, the enemy must fall.
We've been called into the kingdom
For such a time as this.

The Anointing's Flowing

The anointing's flowing from Emmanuel's head
And running down his garment.
It will set you free,
It will bless your soul.
The anointing's flowing today.

Step into the flow
Of the anointing,
That thirst quenching
Soul cleansing flow.
Let him set you free,
Let him bless your soul.
The anointing's flowing today.

We are the vessels,
You are the oil, overflow.

The anointing's flowing today.

There Is A Way

There is a way that seems right unto man
But the end there of is death and destruction.
Lean not unto your own understanding
But lean and depend on God.

He will not fail you,
He will guide you on your way,
He will show you a brighter day,
Just lean and depend on God.

There is a way that leads to destruction,
There's a way that leads to death and hell.
Follow Jesus for he is the answer.
Heaven and earth will pass
But God's word will never fail.

Expectancy

I have an expectancy about the things
God's promised me.
What an expectancy.
I'm like a child on Christmas Eve
Awaiting the Christmas toys,
Like a bride on the eve of marriage
Expecting a lifetime of joy,
Like a mother expecting her first child,
Like a daddy when it' a boy.

I have an expectancy, such an expectancy.

He's given me joy,
Joy, unspeakable joy,
Given me peace that surpasses all understanding,
Given me life abundantly,
Given me Love, so undeserving.

But still there's an expectancy
About the things God's promised me,
Such an expectancy.

He promised to return and receive me one day.
Yes, then I'll see him face to face.
He promised to prepare a place for me,
In a glorious mansion I'll live for eternity.
Wow! What an expectancy

The One Who Reigns

He's El Shadi,
The many breasted one.
He's Jehovah Jirah,
He's our provider.

He's Jehovah Nissi,
He is our banner.
He's Jehovah Shalom,
He gives us peace.

He's Alpha and Omega
The beginning and the end.
He's God Almighty,
All power is in his hands.

He reigns forever,
From the rising of the sun
'Til the going down of the same,
My God, He reigns.

Soon Coming King

I humble myself before the throne of mercy,
Release all that's within.
I open my heart to receive his word,
Richness of his spirit and life.

He satisfies my longing soul,
He fills the hunger within,
Leads me forth with a strong hand,
He delivers me from fear and doubt.

He's my deliverer,
My savior,
My conqueror,
Soon coming King.

You Are My Everything

You are the sunshine
On a cloudy day.
You are the stars that brighten up
The darkest night.

You are the laughter
That drives the frown away.
You are the voice I hear
That makes everything alright.

Wouldn't know what to do without you,
Wouldn't know which way to turn.
I couldn't live without you
For you are my everything.

Wouldn't know how to love without you,
Wouldn't know how to give without you,
There is no hope without,
For you are my everything.

Emerged In You

Our toes are getting wet,
Our feet are not in yet,
But Lord we long to be
Emerged in you.

Help us launch into the deep,
We're seeking you.
We desire the true treasures
Our hearts pursue.

Reveal your secret places,
Show us your wondrous sites,
Let us experience your greatness,
Take us to higher heights.

We want to be emerged in you.

You Are

I feel your Holy presence every moment I'm awake.
I love to walk hand in hand to look upon your face.
I know you're always with me and
That you truly care,
'Cause in my darkest hour your
Presence is still there.

You are my light, my strength, my shield,
My hope, my love, my joy fulfilled;
You're the one who satisfies my needs.
Yes, you're the one who satisfies my needs.

You are my inspiration, you are my friend,
You are my provider, on whom I can depend.
You are my righteousness, you are my peace,
You are my protection against the enemy.

You are my light, my strength, my shield,
My hope, my love, my joy fulfilled.
You're the one who satisfies my needs.
Yes, you're the one who satisfies my needs.

If You Can See What I See

If you can see what I see you will believe;
Believe in the father, believe in the son,
Goodness and mercy wrapped into one.
If you can see what I see
You will believe.

I see creation eagerly awaiting
The hour of jubilee.
I see angelic hosts
Standing at every post;
Nations arising taking territory.

I see heaven opening, I see blessings flowing,
I see captives being set free.
I hear God's word spoken,
I hear the chains being broken,
I hear warriors shouting victory.

If you can see what I see you will believe.

Change

Our hearts have been waiting,
Secretly anticipating
This hour of awakening;
Change is here.

We're synchronized for Miracles,
Synchronized for Health,
Synchronized for Harvest,
Synchronized for Wealth;
Change is here.

Change agents
Get ready to shift,
Coming out of Egypt,
Strengthened with might.
Put on your new garments,
Darkness has turned to light.

Get ready, get ready,
Change is here!
Now walk in it.

Oh Everlasting Flame

Oh everlasting flame
Touch the dark and deepened core
Of my soul; let brightness glow
From your eternal flow,
Oh everlasting flame.

Touch the brittle, cracked marrow
Of my being; enlighten
With healing fire,
Consume all wounds
Making whole my desire.

Arise, lover of my soul.
Awaken the part never exposed
Lest I should sleep continually
Never to know the healing flow
That lives within me.

Oh everlasting flame
Kindle the sparks of my soul
With increased intensity
Until the fire explodes
And others see you in me.

He Satisfies

A life time of searching couldn't fill the void within.
Journeys and expectations proved
fruitless and vain.
Wandering aimlessly trying to find self-worth;
Companions nor friends, fortune nor fame
Could ease the pain.

Then I met him, who called me by name,
Filled me with his love, took away the pain.
He satisfies!

He turned my stony heart into a heart of flesh,
He took my weary soul into a place of rest.
Now, I'm satisfied, showered from above,
Saturated with his presence,
Rescued by his love.
He satisfies!

No Place Like The Bosom of Jesus

There is no place like the bosom of Jesus.
I lay my head upon his breast,
He whispers sweet words in my ear,
Child, I love you, draw near.

There is no place like the bosom of Jesus.
There I find rest, upon his breast,
Peace and joy, love I've never known
There in the bosom of Jesus

There is no place, like the bosom of Jesus.
As he holds me close, his mysteries unfold;
I see his Glory and all his splendor.
I enter in, I enter in.

It's Only Temporary

It's only temporary,
What you're going through.
It's only temporary,
My God sees you,
It's only temporary,
Your hurt and pain
It's only temporary,
New heights you'll gain.

If you stay in the fight,
Keep the faith,
God will give you amazing grace.
You've got to hold on,
God's word is true.
If you keep the faith
He'll deliver you.
This is only temporary.

Thank God for Deliverance

I could feel my feet slip;
I was going down, down.
I could hear the enemy laughing
Then I heard the trumpet sound.
I was wandering aimlessly
But your love has set me free,
Plucked me from the miry clay,
Understanding showed me the way.

Just when I thought the darkness would last
You showed up and brightened my path
Lifted me from a mind of defeat
Never more inclined to repeat

Now I'm on a road that's filled
With all the goodness life can give
Peace and joy now fills my day.
Thank God deliverance came my way.

Distribution Center Arise

Arise, shine, the light has come.
Stand, show forth the salvation of God.
The kingdom in you
Wants to manifest through you.
Distribution Center Arise.

God's reach is broad,
His hunger great.
Release the knowledge,
Unleash your faith,
Distribution Center Arise.

Understand the time and season,
Know today is the day.
The Heavens are open upon you,
His anointing's leading the way.
Distribution Center Arise.

The spot light is on you.
Tell his amazing story,
The captives are waiting.
Reveal his awesome Glory,
Distribution Center Arise.

Take Time to Know Me

Men are running to and fro
Heaping up things on this earth;
Houses and lands, cars and boats,
Trying to find self-worth.

But none of these things will satisfy
The emptiness inside.
The Holy Spirit is crying out
If you want to be satisfied.

Take time to know me,
God's heart is carrying out,
Know me, know me.

Seek first God's kingdom
And his righteousness
And everything, every need,
Every desire your heart possess
Will be added to you.

His heart is crying out
Know me, Know me.

The Anointing

The time is coming,
And yet is now,
When all that hear and obey
Shall taste and be consumed
With his anointing fire;
The anointing that flows from on high.

Our ears will hear,
Our eyes will see
Our hearts will receive
The anointing.

Wake Up

Wake up! Wake up!
It's time to wake up.
Do you know what time it is?
It's time to awaken to the times.

Look around you, what do you see?
To long we've been sleeping,
Blinded by the night;
It's time to awaken to the times.

Pull the scales off your eyes, see what I see;
No more division, only unity.
We've been given riches, not poverty.
It's time to awaken to the times

Prayer

Come, O' fire, purge
With your sacrificial flame,
Let my soul be an offering to your name.

Help me to see with your eyes, feel with your heart.
Giver of blessings pour down.
Eternal Lover, I'm your beloved.

Prepare my heart to pray, as your ears hear.
Prepare my heart to hunger, as your hands fill.
Embody me with the presence of your love.

Jesus My Hero

Jesus is my hero, he fights my every battle.
I'm always a winner because Jesus is my hero.

I am victorious through faith.
The Lord has given me the neck of the enemy,
No weapon formed against me shall prosper
Because my eldest brother Jesus fights for me.

Yes, I am victorious through faith.
Every tongue that rises shall be condemned.
I am mightier than the mightiest
Because I've learned to put my trust in him.

Holy Spirit Fill This Place

Holy Spirit, fill this place
Like you did so long ago
On the day of Pentecost.
We cannot know which way to go
Until you fill this place.

Holy Spirit, fill this place
Like you did so long ago,
We need you now even more;
Reveal yourself as before
On the day of Pentecost.

Victory

I'm walking in the anointing,
Living in Liberty;
The chains of sin are broken,
I've got the victory.
My eldest brother, Jesus,
Paid the price for me;
He took the keys of death and hell
And gave me the victory.

I am victorious through faith,
The Lord has given me the neck of the enemy.
No weapons formed against me shall prosper,
The chains of sin are broken;
God has given me the victory.

That We Might Know Him

That we might know him and his wondrous
working power;
He created the world in six days,
Placed the stars up in the sky,
Divided the waters from dry land,
Created the birds to fly.

And if that wasn't enough
He looked down on his creation and said,
I think I'll make me a man
In the likeness of our image
That he might know me
And my wondrous working power.

He parted the Red Sea,
Raised Lazarus from the dead,
Walked upon the water,
Fed thousands with two fishes
And five loaves of bread

That we might know him
And his wondrous working power.

About the Author

Elois Fuller

is a successful realtor and a married mother of five. She has been blessed with thirteen grandchildren and three great-grandkids.

A lifelong learner who strives to continuously grow personally and professionally, Elois is a Certified Public Speaker who shares her passion and her wisdom to inspire others and support people in living their best life. She lives in South Florida and enjoys music, writing, sports and anointed church meetings.

Contact Elois at
PoetryandMusicfortheSoul@gmail.com
PoetryandMusicfortheSoul.com

PoetryandMusicfortheSoul.com

www.ingramcontent.com/pod-product-compliance
Lightning Source LLC
Chambersburg PA
CBHW071021040426
42443CB00007B/884

9780692600153